Circus

Circus Clown ABC

Denise M. Jordan

Heinemann Library
Chicago, Illinois

Customer Service 888-454-2279
Visit our website at www.heinemannlibrary.com

Designed by Sue Emerson, Heinemann Library
Printed and bound in the U.S.A. by Lake Book

06 05
10 9 8 7 6 5 4 3 2

Library of Congress Cataloging-in-Publication Data
Jordan, Denise M.
   Circus Clown ABC / Denise Jordan.
       p. cm. — (Circus)
Includes index.
Summary: An alphabet book that presents facts about circus clowns.
   ISBN: 1-58810-546-6 (HC), 1-58810-754-X (Pbk.)
   1. Circus—Juvenile literature. 2. Alphabet books. [1. Circus. 2.
   Clowns. 3. Alphabet.] I. Title.
   GV1817 .J672 2002
   791.3—dc21

                                   2001004794

Acknowledgments
The author and publishers are grateful to the following for permission to reproduce copyright material:
p. 3 Layne Kennedy/Corbis; p. 4 Bettmann/Corbis; pp. 5, 17 Eugene G. Schulz; p. 6 PhotoDisc; pp. 7, 21 Scott McKiernan/ZUMA Press; p. 8 N & J Wiseman/Trip; p. 9 Bill Bachmann/rightimage.com; p. 10 Jon Silla/Transparencies, Inc.; p. 11 National Geographic Society; pp. 12, 20 Greg Williams/Heinemann Library; p. 13 Chuck Fishman/Contact Press Images/PictureQuest; p. 14 Michael Gadomski/Earth Scenes; p. 15 J. Ringland/Trip; pp. 16, 19 Jane Faircloth/Transparencies, Inc.; p. 18 Aneal Vohra/Unicorn Stock Photos; p. 22 Bruce Coleman Inc.

Cover photographs courtesy of (L-R): National Geographic Society; J. Ringland/Trip; Greg Williams/Heinemann Library

Every effort has been made to contact copyright holders of any material reproduced in this book. Any omissions will be rectified in subsequent printings if notice is given to the publisher.

Special thanks to our advisory panel for their help in the preparation of this book:

Eileen Day, Preschool Teacher
Chicago, IL

Paula Fischer, K–1 Teacher
Indianapolis, IN

Sandra Gilbert,
Library Media Specialist
Houston, TX

Angela Leeper,
Educational Consultant
North Carolina Department
of Public Instruction
Raleigh, NC

Pam McDonald, Reading Teacher
Winter Springs, FL

Melinda Murphy,
Library Media Specialist
Houston, TX

Helen Rosenberg, MLS
Chicago, IL

Anna Marie Varakin,
Reading Instructor
Western Maryland College

The publishers would also like to thank Fred Dahlinger, Jr., Director of Collections and Research at the Circus World Museum in Baraboo, Wisconsin, and Smita Parida for their help in reviewing the contents of this book.

Some words are shown in bold, **like this.**
You can find them in the picture glossary on page 23.

A a   Alley
B b   Baggy
C c   Clown

Clown alley is where clowns get dressed.

Clowns wear baggy clothes.

D d   Dog

Some clowns work with dogs.

E e Eye
F f Face

Clowns use their eyes to look happy or sad.

Clowns paint their faces with bright colors.

G g   Glove
H h   Hand

Clowns wear gloves.

You can see their hands from far away.

I i   Inside

This clown is inside a shoe.

Jj   Juggle

Clowns **juggle.**

K k   Kid
L l   Laugh

Clowns make kids laugh.

M m   Mime

Clowns mime.

They act out words.

N n   Nose

Clowns wear big, red noses.

O o   Officer
P p   Police

Police officers try to catch the bad guys.

Q q   Quiet

Some clowns are quiet.

They don't toot noisy horns.

R r Ruff

ruff

Some clowns wear **ruffs.**

Ruffs are big, fluffy collars.

S s Silly Shoe Sock

Most clowns wear big, silly shoes.

They wear bright, colorful socks.

T t   Trick

Some clowns do magic tricks.

U u   Umbrella

This clown has a tiny umbrella.

V v   Voice

Clowns don't use their voices.

They toot horns or mime.

W w　Wig

wig

Clowns wear funny **wigs** and hats.

X x Exciting

The circus is exciting.

Clowns make the circus fun.

Yy Young

Young children can be clowns, too.

Z z   Zip

Clowns zip around the **ring**.

Picture Glossary

clown alley
page 3

ruff
page 14

juggle
page 8

wig
page 19

ring
page 22

Note to Parents and Teachers

Using this book, children can practice alphabetic skills while learning interesting facts about the circus. Together, read *Circus Clown ABC.* Say the names of the letters aloud, then say the target word, exaggerating the beginning of the word. For example, "/r/: Rrrr-uff." Can the child think of any other words that begin with the /r/ sound? (Although the letter x is not at the beginning of the word "exciting," the /ks/ sound of the letter x is still prominent.) Try to sing the "ABC song," substituting the circus clown alphabet words for the letters a, b, c, and so on.

Index